Socially Sober

Beyond the Bottle: One Woman's Journey to Thriving Without Alcohol

Nikki Delgado

Contents

Introduction

I'll never forget the morning after my friend's 40th birthday. It hadn't been a wild night - just a few drinks over several hours. But the next day, I felt as though I'd been hit by a train. A pounding headache, nausea and exhaustion stole the day I had planned to spend with my kids. As I lay on the couch, I realised something: alcohol no longer agreed with me. What had once been a way to relax was now leaving me drained, taking more than it gave.

I had always considered myself healthy - working out most days and eating clean, but alcohol was the one thing that didn't fit into that picture. I had tried taking breaks before and felt great each time, but I always went back to drinking, telling myself it wasn't that big of a deal. Yet, the older I got, the more obvious it became that alcohol wasn't adding to my life - it was stealing from it.

Then, something happened that really shifted my perspective. It wasn't a hangover or an embarrassing night out, but a moment that shook me to my core and made me question the role alcohol played in my life. That day set me on a path I hadn't anticipated, a journey that would lead me to question whether alcohol had any place in my future at all. I will go into more detail about this in Chapter 2, where I explore the events and emotions that finally pushed me to reconsider my relationship with alcohol.

It wasn't an overnight decision to quit forever but over time the idea of drinking started to feel more and more irrelevant. Why would I go back to something that made me feel worse?

Why Sobriety and Socialising Matter

One of the most difficult parts about quitting alcohol is not the actual giving up, it's the social pressure that surrounds it. Alcohol is tightly knitted into our social lives. It's at the centre of celebrations, events and even casual get-togethers with friends. It's a common factor in most social events and when you choose to take a step away from it, you can often feel like an outsider.

For many people, alcohol feels like a social boost, something that takes the edge off the anxious feelings and makes conversations flow more easily. It helps people to feel more relaxed, more comfortable and more confident in social situations.

So, when you decide to stop drinking, you are not just opting out of alcohol, you are opting out of the societal norms that go with it. You will become the odd one out who isn't participating in toasts, the one who says "just a sparkling water for me" at the bar, and sometimes that can feel isolating. It can also make others feel uncomfortable. People will ask questions, maybe even challenge your decision, because alcohol is so ingrained in their own lives.

For me, socialising without alcohol was a learning curve and this is one of the reasons I felt so passionate about writing this book. I wanted others to learn and grow from my experiences and to know that they can have the confidence and self-belief to be socially sober.

The first few times I went on nights out without drinking I felt a little out of place. I wasn't used to being the only sober person in the room. I was feeling worried within myself about how people would look at me. "Nikki is the party girl" or "she's the wild one". I think people just expected me to have a drink. Would I still be "fun" if I didn't have a drink and how would people judge me?

But something amazing happened over time. I began to enjoy social events even more without alcohol. I was fully present, able to engage in conversations with a clear mind and not stumble over my words (something that used to happen often).

I found that I could connect more deeply with people around me and I wasn't reliant on alcohol to loosen up or enjoy myself. It was just the real me and that was enough! I didn't need that layer of alcohol anymore, I just showed up as myself.

This book is all about navigating the social landscape while sober. I am so passionate about how my life has changed since I quit alcohol that I wanted to write this book to help others do the same.

I want to help you find ways to remain true to your own personal decision to be sober while still fully participating in life. Quitting alcohol is not about shutting yourself away from the world to avoid temptation and questions.

While it's not easy, it is so incredibly rewarding. My goal is to share my own story with you, my own beautiful and challenging experiences, and offer you practical guidance and tips to help you along the way.

Whether you are just thinking about cutting back or are ready to embrace sobriety for the long haul, this book is here to show you that it's absolutely possible to live a full, rich, exciting and beautiful life without alcohol.

Who This Book Is For

This book is for those who find themselves in the middle lane of drinking—the sober curious, grey area drinkers and anyone contemplating a change in their relationship with alcohol for the sake of their health and well-being.

It's not intended for those struggling with alcoholism or addiction, but rather for individuals who are questioning the role alcohol plays in their lives.

If you've ever wondered whether alcohol is truly adding value to your life or felt that subtle, nagging sense that you might be better off without it, this book is for you. My journey isn't about hitting rock bottom or battling addiction; it's about realising that life might actually be better, brighter and more beautiful without alcohol in the picture.

This is not a guide filled with rigid rules or dramatic declarations about quitting forever. It's a story you can resonate with, a journey of self-discovery and mindful choices.

Whether you're already exploring sobriety or simply curious about how removing alcohol could transform your life, my hope is that by sharing my experiences you'll feel empowered to start your own journey.

The goal is to help you reflect, consider and find your own version of freedom without alcohol.

What You Will Gain From This Book as a Reader

Throughout this book I will take you along on my journey - one that begins with my life before sobriety and continues through the stages of quitting and learning to thrive without alcohol. Each chapter will offer my personal experiences along with practical advice and tips to help guide you on your own sober journey, whether you are considering a temporary break or taking on my First 100 Days Sober Challenge.

In Chapter 1 we will dive deep into the role that alcohol played in my life when I was drinking. How it shaped my social life, how it affected my relationships and shaped my lifestyle. I will share stories from my own experiences and also the moment when I began to question the value alcohol had in my life.

Chapter 2 will focus on the turning point for me - the moment when I realised that I needed to make a change. I will also explore the doubts and fears that come with making such a decision. I will offer insights into difficult conversations I had with friends and family about my choice to quit drinking and how you can approach these moments in your own situation.

Chapter 3 is all about my early days of sobriety - some of the challenges I faced with breaking old habits, overcoming social awkwardness on nights out and socialising with friends sober. I will also discuss the strategies I used to stay on track.

In Chapter 4 I will explore the incredible and life changing benefits that have come with quitting alcohol. Think better sleep, weight loss and clear skin to name just a few. I will share with you how living without alcohol has transformed my relationships and outlook on life along with all the beautiful things I have discovered for myself.

Chapter 5 will cover the practical side of sobriety in social situations. How to prepare yourself for social events, how to handle pressure from friends and family, as well as how to find new ways to enjoy being social without alcohol.

I'll give you all the tools and strategies you will need to believe in yourself and help you stay confident and connected, even in situations where everyone else is drinking. I'll share with you some practical tips for navigating the world of socialising without alcohol and how to handle moments of temptation.

Finally, in Chapter 6 I will introduce you to my First 100 Days Sober Challenge, a transformative program that allows you to experience life without alcohol. I will walk you through the process of committing to the challenge, how to track your progress, and the milestones to celebrate along the way. This chapter is about embracing your own personal journey and discovering all the beautiful life changes that come along with living your life socially sober.

At the end of Chapter 6 I have included a bonus workbook section to accompany you on the challenge. This includes prompts designed to help you integrate the challenge into your life. Fill in as much or as little as you like but most importantly, enjoy the process of reflection, gratitude and celebrations of your achievements.

How to Use This Book

I wrote this book not only to share my personal experiences with socialising sober but also to provide you with practical tools and strategies to begin your own sobriety journey, whether you are sober-curious or are seeking to strengthen your commitment to an alcohol-free lifestyle.

Here is how to make the most of this book:

Read at your own pace: The first 4 chapters are about my own story and experience. Each chapter is structured to be read alone, which allows you to jump to the sections that most resonate with you. While I encourage you to read them in sequence, feel free to revisit specific chapters or topics if needed.

1. Create your own personal plan: Using the advice and hacks in Chapter 5 you will be ready to take on the challenge in Chapter 6.
2. Engage in the workbook sections: At the end of the book, I have put together a workbook to help you on your own sobriety journey. Fill in as much or as little as you feel necessary for your own journey.
3. Reflect and journal: At the end of the book, I will prompt you to reflect on your thoughts and feelings during your journey. Take time to journal your responses and practice gratitude throughout your challenge. These practices have really helped me in my journey and I hope they will help you as well.
4. Practice self-compassion: Sobriety is a personal journey, and it's important to approach it with kindness towards yourself. Celebrate milestones and successes throughout the journey and don't be too hard on yourself if you encounter difficulties along the way. Growth takes time and practice. Always put progress before perfection.

5. Stay open-minded: Be willing and open to exploring new ideas, creating new habits and trying new activities along the way. Embrace the changes and obstacles you may meet and allow yourself to grow throughout the process.

This book is your companion for navigating social situations without alcohol. It is all about discovering the beauty of real life without the coating of alcohol to mask it. Once you switch your mindset and begin your own journey you will find that it's not only possible to live without drinking - it's all about thriving beyond that bottle.

You will come away from this book with the tools, confidence and inspiration to begin your own sobriety journey. Whether that means cutting back, taking a break or beginning your own long-term journey I am here to support you.

Chapter 1
Life Under the Influence

Early Days of Drinking

For as long as I can remember alcohol was always around, a pretty much constant part of my life since I was a teenager. At first it felt like an exciting new discovery, a rite of passage that me and all of my friendship group embraced. It was a symbol of being a grown up and I remember my parents encouraging me to have an alcopop or two at Christmas.

On nights out with my school friends, drinking wasn't just an activity, it was the main event. On weekends we would spend hours getting ready to go out to a nightclub, drinking cheap vodka and orange juice at each other's houses. Not just a couple of drinks though, we would sometimes drink until we were sick before we even went out. The goal wasn't just to have fun, it was to get drunk.

As a teenager, I didn't even realise there was another way to drink. Moderation was never part of the conversation, but excess always was. We laughed off our hangovers, even as they made us throw up and suffer the next morning. This was a small price to pay for the "fun" we'd had the night before. I even remember laughing about an event where one of my friends had to have her stomach pumped in hospital because she was so drunk. Everyone drank that way. We felt invincible and no one told us otherwise, so we never questioned it at the time.

When I look back it is difficult to figure out the exact moment when drinking stopped being fun and started to feel like more of a burden. In my teenage years, drinking was all about excitement and new found freedom but it had also become a necessity to socialise.

It was not even something you did for fun anymore - it was something you did to fit in. If you didn't drink, you were cast out. The pressure to fit in as a teenager was immense, especially as a girl. Alcohol held together the socialising and it was never something I even thought about not doing.

The Social Circle of Alcohol

By the time I had entered my late teens, drinking had become a regular habit. It was a way of life. It wasn't just the occasional party or celebration, it was part of every social event. Friendships involved alcohol and it was a currency of connection with others. If I wanted to be part of a group I had to drink. So I did, and I did it again, and again.

It's strange to think back at how normalised this behaviour was. I worked in a restaurant and a bar in my late teens and was surrounded with alcohol. Of course, when the night's work finished, we would start drinking ourselves, often in a club or another late-night drinking venue and carry on until the early hours.

Weekends were spent hopping from bar to bar, downing cocktails and shots, and laughing about the craziness of it all. The more we drank, the better the night seemed - until the next morning of course. But being young, we brushed off the hangovers and temporary discomforts. The headaches and sickness were all just part of the experience, something to laugh about the next day.

Hangovers were almost like a badge of honour. The worse we felt, the more fun we must have had the night before. At least that is what we told ourselves. Suffering was worn almost like a trophy, with no time spared to consider what we were doing to our bodies – we were living in the moment.

The Stage School Years: Balancing Training and Drinking

At age 18 I was accepted into stage school in London. The training was incredibly demanding, both physically and mentally. I would train daily for hours on end, starting at 8 in the morning and finishing in the evening, with classes in dancing, acting and singing. My body was pushed to its limits and on school days there was no space for drinking.

During the week I would be so disciplined, going to bed early and resting in the evenings. I knew that I couldn't perform well if I was hungover or sleep deprived. But on Friday or Saturday nights, it was a different story. I would meet up with my friends from home and hit the bars again. I would drink to excess, throwing back drinks as if they were water and by Sunday, I would find myself flaked out on the sofa in a miserable hungover slump.

This cycle repeated for the next three years - Monday through Friday, I was focussed on my training, working hard and determined. But as soon as the weekend rolled around, I would fall back to the binge drinking habits. It didn't occur to me that there might be another way. That was how life was, working hard during the week, partying hard on the weekends and suffering the consequences later. I felt comfortable in this routine - it was just normal to me.

The Professional World: Drinking Lifestyle

After graduating from stage school, I was offered my first dancing contract in a show in Rhodes, Greece. The show was hard and demanding, and it took me a while to get used to the heat. We were based in the middle of a party island so every night, once the shows were finished, we would head to one of the local bars or clubs and the drinking would start. After every performance there was an unspoken expectation that we would go out to celebrate.

Food was often an afterthought in those years. A snack here and there, and Greek salads to keep the alcohol from hitting too hard, but the drinking was a constant. It was the lifestyle - one that seemed glamorous on the surface, but underneath it was exhausting and destructive. Looking back on it I'm not sure how I managed to get through that first contract with the demands I placed on my body.

I remember one night in particular, after a show I drank far too much and ended up getting on the back of a motorbike with someone I barely knew. I was very drunk and needed to be sick.

When I got back to our apartment, I remember getting in the shower to try and sober myself up, only to end up lying down half asleep with the water still running. Looking back on this memory I realise that I am lucky to be alive. When I woke up the next morning, I felt horrible and I looked at myself in the mirror and swore that I wouldn't let it happen again. But I knew that at the end of the day there would be another show, another celebration and another reason to drink again.

Dependence on Alcohol

As the years went by and I slid into my twenties I began to notice something unsettling, alcohol wasn't just something that I was enjoying socially anymore. It had become something that I enjoyed doing on my own.

It wasn't just for parties or big social events anymore. It was slowly creeping into more and more aspects of my life. I found myself reaching for a drink after a stressful day, using alcohol as a way to relax and unwind. It had slowly snuck into my daily habits in ways that I didn't even realise at the time.

It was only a drink or two at a time but while drinking alone had previously been unusual for me, it was now turning into a more regular habit. A glass of wine while cooking dinner or a vodka with sparkling water in the garden while reading. It all seemed harmless enough, but it was adding up.

I wasn't drinking to get drunk at that time, I was drinking to take the edge off a stressful day, just to slightly blur the lines of reality. Alcohol had become a crutch for me and I was leaning on it more than I cared to admit.

The toll it was taking on my body was undeniable. I had started to notice that my sleep was suffering. Even after a couple of drinks I would find myself waking up at 4am on the dot most nights - sweating, grinding my teeth and feeling anxious.

Sometimes my heart would be racing and my body would be crying out for hydration. My energy levels had started to drop and I found myself skipping my morning workouts - often feeling too exhausted to do them. Not only that, I found that my weight was creeping up, despite feeling like I was eating healthily most of the time. I know looking back I wasn't always making the best food choices when I was drinking. Oftentimes wine led to crisps, cheese and other salty snacks.

The Cost of Drinking: Physical Toll

The hangovers became harder and harder to ignore. When I was younger, I could easily bounce back from a night of heavy drinking. But as I was getting older, the hangovers were becoming more intense and seemed to last longer. It wasn't just a headache the next day anymore.

I found that drinking was making me feel tired and affecting my sleep throughout the week, even if I only had a couple of glasses of wine. I was struggling to get through the week, only to repeat the cycle come Friday evening.

Along with the stubborn weight gain I started to notice that my skin was in a terrible state. I developed a patch of red rosacea on the side of my face that I just couldn't shift. I blamed it on makeup products, spf and even stress.

At this point I began to realise that alcohol wasn't really adding anything positive to my life. It was only taking things away. Time spent recovering from hangovers was interfering with my workouts, my healthy food choices and productive work hours, not to mention the time I should have spent doing something meaningful with friends and family. Yet I wasn't ready to completely break free from alcohol.

The "Mummy Needs Wine" Culture

As my 30's passed by it wasn't just special occasions and celebrations where I was drinking. It had become a regular habit. Especially once I moved to Spain. The "mummy needs wine" culture was everywhere and I became a part of it without even realising. It wasn't about getting drunk to excess anymore, it was about a glass of wine to take the edge off a stressful day. A drink at the end of the week to celebrate the weekend. A reward after a week of juggling work with kids and everything else.

I was definitely not alone in this, everywhere I looked it was reinforced. Social media was full of memes and reels on how a glass of wine was a mum's best friend, how if she survived the chaos of family life, she deserved that large glass of wine at the end of the day.

There were novelty wine glasses that could hold an entire bottle of wine, marketed as funny gifts for overworked mums. I would joke with friends about it being wine o'clock and how we all needed a glass of wine after the kids were in bed to cope with the bedtime battles. It seemed harmless enough. We were all in the same position after all.

But the truth was this was just another technique I used to normalise drinking. A way for it to feel like less of a problem and more of an essential. "Mummy needs wine" wasn't just a joke anymore, it was becoming part of who I was. I would have that glass, sometimes two, not because I really wanted it but because I felt I deserved it. I was stressed, tired and overextended, and wine seemed like an easy solution. It was how I unwound, how I escaped, even if it was only for a little while.

Friday night drinking would become a regular routine, even meeting with friends straight after school for the essential glass of wine. It was the signal that the week was finally over and I could relax. But soon it wasn't just Fridays. In the summer holidays of 2022, I decided I was going to have a relaxing summer and not even think too much about working out or worry about what I ate or drank. I must have had a glass of wine most nights and by the time September rolled around I felt horrible. Lazy, lethargic and a few kilos heavier than I'd been before.

This habit was something I could easily laugh off, after all I was just blowing off some steam after a long day and everyone else was doing it, right? I started to notice how much I was looking forward to that glass of wine at the end of the day, and I would feel disappointed if I felt I could not have it. It was often a topic of conversation with friends as well.

At the time it seemed like harmless fun. But looking back, I can see how alcohol was seeping into every corner of my life. It was not just about celebrating, or even socialising - it was about coping with life. The more I leaned into the "mummy needs wine" story, the more I realised that the joke was turning into a problem.

Dry January: Reaping the Benefits but Not Ready to Let Go

In 2019 I decided to make a shift with my health and started eating in a cleaner, more whole foods style way. For the first 30 days I challenged myself to follow the Whole 30 program - a complete elimination diet, removing certain foods to see how my body would respond when everything was stripped back. Alcohol being one of the things I removed.

I had heard people rave about how this challenge helped to reset their system, clear their minds and shed unwanted weight. I wanted to see how it would affect my body and mind. Deep down I knew I wasn't entirely ready to give up alcohol completely, but 30 days seemed like a good place to start.

The first few days were tough - there were times I went out with friends without drinking, explaining I was on a 30-day cleanse, which people seemed to understand. As the days went on, I started to feel amazing. My energy levels increased and I was waking up feeling ready to work out each morning. My sleep improved and I wasn't waking up at 4am sweating and anxious. I felt great!

I felt clear minded and fresh, and even the skin on my face started to look brighter and clearer. The weight started to come off without the evening wine and snacks. I felt that I was finally taking control of my body and my health, and could see myself sticking with this style of eating going forwards, but I wasn't sure if I was ready to give up alcohol for good just yet.

As the 30 days came to an end, I felt a huge sense of pride and accomplishment. But I also felt the need to reward myself with a drink for doing so well. And that is exactly what I did. I celebrated with a friend the next day with a glass of wine.

For the first time in my life other than pregnancy I'd had a taste of what life could be like without alcohol. During the 30 days I wasn't just surviving without it, I was thriving. I felt stronger, more in tune with my body and in many ways, more alive. Yet despite all this, a part of me wasn't ready to say goodbye to it just yet. I knew my body felt amazing eating this way and I thought I could maintain a healthy life by eating well and having an occasional drink here and there.

I thought that I could reintroduce alcohol in moderation. I told myself I would stay under control. In my mind, wine was a pretty natural alcohol, right? And vodka with sparkling water was a clean drink, no? I told myself I would just drink on special occasions but the reality was that it didn't take long before old habits started to creep back in. The occasional drink turned into a regular one. Weekends became an excuse to indulge again, and before I knew it, I was back to where I'd started.

The difference now was that I was maintaining my clean eating lifestyle, so because my body was clean, every time I drank alcohol it was rejecting it even more than before I did the Whole 30. Drinking was making me feel worse than ever. On nights out I was finding that after just a few drinks I would be sick, and even after a single glass of wine my body would feel exhausted the next day.

Along with the alcohol came the weight I had lost during the Whole 30 challenge. Despite maintaining a clean diet, it was slowly sneaking back on. Once again, my sleep started to suffer, the nights of tossing and turning returning after every drink. The mental clarity I had built up began to fade again, replaced with the dull fog that alcohol brought with it.

After a few months I remember looking back feeling frustrated with myself for letting it slip away. I knew how great I had felt so I went about repeating the Whole 30 several times more. A

Dry January followed and I would feel great again. I was reaping the benefits of cutting out alcohol even if it was temporary but I still wasn't ready to fully embrace sobriety. Part of me kept holding onto the belief that I could have it both ways. I could enjoy the rewards of sobriety without fully committing to it.

So that was the cycle I found myself in. I would do a drastic challenge like the Whole 30 every few months. The benefits were easy to see, I would feel amazing. But as soon as I finished it and allowed alcohol back into my life everything would start to slip downhill again. It was a frustrating pattern that I would spend years repeating.

Looking back on this I realise that the Whole 30 challenge was truly an eye-opening experience for me. It gave me a glimpse of what life could be like without alcohol. But 30 days simply wasn't long enough to make a lasting habit. I would make excuses not to go out during that time, not to socialise or make plans with friends, and just avoid the wine aisle in the supermarket completely.

The challenge gave me a real taste of the benefits of sobriety but I wasn't ready to embrace them all just yet. I thought I could go back to drinking again each time but every time I did, the same negative consequences followed. It was a lesson that would stay with me, even if I wasn't ready to act on it at that moment.

The Struggle to Break Free

It took me a long time to realise that alcohol was not my friend. What I thought was fun, what I thought was relaxation was actually just bringing more negativity into my life. As my hangovers got worse, and I started to see in the mirror the damage alcohol was doing to my body I began to question what I was doing to myself.

Looking back now, I can see that the signs were always there, I was just not ready to face them. It took years of back and forth, reflection and discovery to finally break free from alcohol and discover life without it. The journey was not always easy, but I truly feel it was one of the most important ones I have ever taken. In the next chapter I will take you through my break free moment, what finally made me decide to quit and the beginning of my sobriety journey.

Chapter 2

The Decision to Change

The Turning Point

As I said in the previous chapter, I had flirted with the idea of giving up alcohol over the previous few years, but it had never stuck. In the periods where I had experimented with cutting out alcohol and doing challenges like Whole30 and Dry January I had felt incredible. My energy levels would be high, I would see a clear up in my skin and I would sleep like an absolute baby. The absence of booze made everything feel sharper and clearer, and I was more productive.

As my food intake became more whole food based, the shift in my diet was monumental. I felt so much healthier, less bloated, more energised and overall just better. With this clean eating diet my body just seemed to reject alcohol whenever I was drinking. It was almost as if my body was clean and it just didn't like that I was putting a poison inside me.

The decision to quit drinking didn't come as one big, dramatic moment. Instead, it happened gradually over a few years as I was more and more aware of my body and how it was reacting to eating and drinking certain things.

But there was one particular moment that solidified my reasons for stopping drinking. One morning, as I was driving home after a Zumba class, I saw a woman get knocked off her moped by a car. I jumped out of my car to help and was the first to call the ambulance.

While we were waiting, I lay on the ground next to her to reassure her that everything would be ok. She had a cut on her head under her helmet but she was conscious and speaking and even laughing at some moments. I got to know her and waited with her until help arrived. I got her name and decided to check in with her to make sure she was ok over the next few days. When the ambulance left I felt a bit shaken up but I was sure she was going to make a full recovery.

A few days later I found out that she had died of a brain bleed and it shook me to my core. I had been on the ground next to her, speaking with her, and it just seemed so unfair that she had died.

I couldn't wrap my head around the accident and it gave me a terrifying glimpse into how fragile life really is. She was 38, the same age I was at that time. I was absolutely devastated, I cannot describe the sadness I felt mourning the life of a woman who was almost a stranger to me, I knew her for less than 30 minutes yet I felt so close and connected to her.

Although alcohol wasn't directly involved in the accident, something clicked in my head and I made a promise to myself. I would never have a drink and get behind the wheel of a car again. I had always stayed under the limit, never more than one glass of wine, but the risk was just not worth it. The thought of putting myself, someone else or my children in danger terrified me. Having a drink and driving was not something I could justify anymore.

From that moment on I began to look at alcohol differently. I started following some accounts on Instagram of other women who were either sober-curious or had quit drinking for good. I was so motivated and inspired by their journeys. At this point, removing it from my life didn't feel like depriving myself of anything anymore. I realised that alcohol had seeped into so many areas of my social life. Once I had committed to not drinking and driving the decision to stop completely seemed to come more naturally.

After the accident, I decided that I would have a longer Dry January that year. I would do 60 days instead of 30. But once I reached the end of my 60 days I realised that I didn't have that same urge to have a drink. I decided to extend it, pushing it further back to my holiday in April instead.

As the weeks turned into months, I found myself in more and more situations where alcohol had always played a role—birthday parties, nights out, date nights and meet-ups with friends. These were the moments I used to think would be the hardest to cope with without a drink in my hand. But something felt different this time, even though I had done Whole 30s before and experienced similar benefits.

The familiar feelings of clarity, energy and control returned, but with more intensity. This time, they were stronger and more lasting. I wasn't just on a temporary break; I was embracing a new way of living, and it felt more sustainable.

What really surprised me was that I didn't miss alcohol at all. I remembered how in previous cleanses, there had always been that nagging sense of deprivation, like I was missing out on something. But this time, it wasn't there. In fact, I was enjoying myself more than ever.

Waking up on a Sunday without a hangover felt revolutionary, just as it had during past detoxes, but now it was becoming a regular part of my life. I found myself buzzing with energy, ready to get a workout in, enjoy the morning or even squeeze in some extra work. In the past, I would have still been in bed, groggy and regretful. The sharpness I had felt during those 30-day breaks was now my everyday reality.

The improvements extended far beyond my mood and energy. My workouts were better and I felt more productive in every area of my life. I was making smarter financial decisions too. Money that would have been spent on drinks, taxis home or late-night food was now being saved or invested elsewhere.

Physically, my body responded positively in every way, just like it had before, but now the changes stuck. I lost the weight I needed to and, for the first time, I kept it off. The persistent red patch on my cheek that had bothered me for so long cleared up and my skin began to glow. The whites of my eyes were clearer and brighter, and friends and family were noticing.

Sleep had always been a struggle when I was drinking, even when I was just having one or two drinks. I remembered the restless nights and the dreaded 4 a.m. wakeups that plagued me after even a couple of drinks. But now, my sleep was deep, peaceful and uninterrupted.

I woke up rested, and the usual stress and anxiety that I hadn't fully recognised before were gone. I was more patient and present with my kids, less irritable and much more engaged in the moment. Looking back, I hadn't realised just how much alcohol had been fuelling the daily stress I had thought was just part of life. In previous breaks, I'd felt some relief, but this time the shift felt profound and permanent.

By removing alcohol, my entire life felt lighter, brighter and far more manageable. My thoughts were clearer, more focused and unclouded by the fog that alcohol had so often brought into my day-to-day life. The familiar feeling of empowerment that I had tasted in past detoxes was now something I lived with daily. And as the benefits continued to stack up, I realised this wasn't just another break.

Never drinking again hadn't been part of my original plan - just like before, I had initially told myself I'd only take a short break - but this time, as the days of sobriety accumulated, the benefits became undeniable.

My life was better in every way, and with each sober day, I knew there was no going back. It wasn't that I was fighting to stay sober; it was that I no longer saw alcohol as something that added any value to my life. The temptation to return to it faded more with each passing day, and I felt stronger than ever in my decision.

Initial Fears and Doubts

When I first committed to not drinking, I had a lot of fears. Even though I had already experienced the benefits of quitting alcohol in my Whole 30s and Dry Januarys, the idea of giving up long term felt a little scary.

One of my biggest fears was that I would be constantly craving that glass of wine, especially in social settings when I saw other people drinking. I was worried that going out without having a drink would feel awkward, I would miss out on the fun, the jokes or even worse, I would be considered the boring one at parties.

There was also a huge part of me that was afraid of missing out. I am definitely a FOMO sufferer and alcohol had been such a big part of my social life for so long I simply couldn't imagine fully letting go of myself without it.

What if I could not loosen up without it? Would I feel out of place at social events where everyone else was drinking? Would I be able to relax and enjoy myself in the same way I had before? The idea of attending events like weddings, birthdays or even casual nights out with friends without drinking felt intimidating and I wasn't sure I would be able to handle it.

On top of that, I was concerned by what other people would think of me. Would people assume I was an alcoholic because I wasn't drinking? Would they label me as a problem drinker? Would they judge me if I didn't drink, would I become the boring friend? I wasn't sure what my identity would be if I didn't drink.

Despite these fears and thoughts, I kept reminding myself why I was doing it. I knew how much better I felt when I wasn't drinking, how much more productive I was, how much more balanced and calm my life had become. And I always had the thought in the back of my head of the accident I had witnessed. Life was short and I needed to experience every beautiful day with a clear mind. This kept me grounded in my decision, even when the doubts started to creep in.

I realised that what I feared most was not the actual lack of alcohol, but the change it would bring. Change is always uncomfortable at first, but I was ready for it.

Telling Friends and Family

Talking to my friends and family about my decision to quit drinking was a little daunting. I knew people would have their opinions, and I wasn't sure how I would explain my decision in a way that didn't feel like a judgement on their drinking habits. Alcohol is so ingrained in our culture that people can get defensive when you talk about the reasons why you aren't drinking. At first, I decided I wasn't going to make a big deal about it, simply telling people I was taking a break from alcohol, not necessarily quitting forever but just taking a step away to focus on my health.

Most of my family were supportive. My dad had stopped drinking at around the same age as me so he backed me in my decision and understood my reasons well. I do remember meeting a little resistance from my mum, who felt as if she had lost her drinking buddy and the first few times we spent time together she noticed she was actively drinking less around me. I told her I wasn't saying never again to alcohol but I wasn't making any plans to start drinking again anytime soon.

Explaining it to my friends was a little more complicated. A lot of my social life had revolved around drinking, and I felt that if I stopped I would be stepping away from something that we shared together. I was worried about how they would react and whether it would change our dynamic. Some of my closest friends were surprised but also curious. They wanted to know why I was making this decision. I could tell they didn't fully understand my reasons at the time. I got responses like "But you will have a drink on your birthday, right?" or "You are not quitting forever, are you?"

They also wanted to know if I was doing it for health reasons or if I had a problem with alcohol. I told them it wasn't about hitting rock bottom, or being an alcoholic but more about how much better I felt without it.

Some of these questions were hard to answer because I didn't know the answers myself. I was not ready to say that I would never drink again. But I did not want to keep explaining and justifying my choice over and over again.

I noticed that when I told people I wasn't drinking, they often felt the need to justify their own drinking habits. They would tell me how they could moderate their drinking if they wanted to, or how they didn't drink that much. It was almost as if my decision not to have a drink made them feel uncomfortable and they needed to defend their own choices.

One of the hardest things to deal with were the assumptions people made. Friends that I wasn't very close to or people I would meet for the first time would assume that I had a problem with alcohol and that was why I had quit, because I could not control myself.

Others thought that it was just a phase and I would eventually go back to drinking like everyone else. While I did get some support from my closest friends, some would casually ask "Can I tempt you with a wine?" or say things like "You used to be so much fun when you were drunk". It stung, even though I know they didn't mean to hurt me.

But the truth was obvious to me. I didn't need alcohol to have fun anymore. That realisation was truly liberating and one of the reasons I wanted to write this book. The more time I spent not drinking, the more I was enjoying social events. I was laughing, dancing, enjoying more meaningful conversations with people and best of all, I was remembering every second of it the next morning.

I certainly wasn't missing the hangovers. I felt in [illegible] life and became confident saying no to alcohol. Once th[illegible] in my head, I found it easy to navigate social situations [illegible] out it.

In Chapter 5 I have put together some Socially Sober Hacks that have worked for me to help you navigate your own social situations. Ideas on what to say when you meet resistance to not drinking, how to organise social events that don't revolve around alcohol and how to navigate situations like a pro.

l Reactions

t sober, the more opportunities to attend
)ped up. I faced them full on and didn't
ıse I wasn't drinking. This was a key part
when I had done 30-day detoxes, or Dry
urposely put off attending events where
drinking would ... ıvolved.

The reactions I got were varied. Some people were supportive and curious, they were genuinely interested in my decision to quit and wanted to know more about the benefits. Others were a little confused, not sure how to process the fact that I wasn't drinking anymore.

Some friends were quick to offer alternatives, suggesting non-alcoholic drinks or mocktails or encouraging me to try something else. But there were also people who seemed to take my decision personally, as though my choice to quit drinking was a direct reflection on them.

In the beginning there were temptations to give in. Attending social events gave me chances to test my will power. At the start, there were moments when I would see others having fun with drinks in hand while I sipped on water or a mocktail, but as the people around me became more and more intoxicated, the more this feeling evaporated.

I was still feeling great and fresh, while the people around me started to look bleary eyed, make-up started to run, their words started to slur and their voices got louder. I would remind myself of how good it would feel to wake up without a hangover the next day and the temptation would gradually slip away.

One of the biggest surprises I noticed in the beginning was how much control I had over my life. Without alcohol I didn't feel tied down to social events. When the others started to get more and more drunk (and annoying) I could simply leave and drive myself home, waking up the next morning feeling fresh. It gave me a real sense of freedom. No more trying to manage how much I was drinking, worrying about a taxi home or dealing with a hangover the next morning. It felt empowering to have full control over my evenings out.

It was eye opening to me how deeply alcohol is woven into our lives. People would often try to tempt me with drinks. It reminded me of how no one would ever offer a cigarette to someone who had quit smoking. Yet with alcohol, the pressure was different. Saying no was sometimes treated as a temporary answer, something that could be changed with enough gentle pressure.

I found that some people needed time to adjust to the idea that I wasn't going to be the same person I was with alcohol, and that was ok. What mattered to me most was that I was becoming the best version of myself. As time went on, I found that the decision to quit alcohol wasn't just about removing something negative, it was about making more space for everything special and beautiful that life had to offer.

Chapter 3
Embracing Sobriety

The First Few Weeks

The first few weeks after deciding to quit alcohol were a bit of a mix of emotions and challenges. While the decision itself felt empowering, I hadn't realised before just how normal alcohol was in social events. The habitual nature of drinking wasn't something I had really considered until I faced the reality of living without it. I was not just cutting out alcohol, I was changing the way I was socialising, and even my personality at social events.

In the beginning when a Friday night would roll around, I felt like there was a gap in my routine where a glass of wine or two used to be. It was not the physical craving that hit me hardest but the ritual of having a drink that surprised me.

The social pressure was also something that I hadn't been prepared for. Almost every time I socialised I would find myself in situations where alcohol was not just present but expected. Friends were planning birthdays, dinners out and Friday afternoons on the beach, all of which involved alcohol. In those first few weeks, I worried that without drinking I might lose my connection with these social groups, people would stop inviting me, or I would lose some of my friends completely.

There was a moment in the first few weeks when I was sitting at a friend's birthday party surrounded by people who were laughing and drinking. At that moment, I wondered if I would ever be able to enjoy social occasions as much as I had when I was drinking. Would I ever be able to feel comfortable and relaxed without alcohol?

Emotionally, the first few weeks were a mix of both pride and fear. I felt proud of myself for making this major life change and I was reaping the benefits, but there was an underlying fear that I wouldn't be able to stick to it.

Every social event felt like a test to me, could I handle being around people who were drinking without giving in and having a drink? Would I actually be able to enjoy myself if I was sober? The truth was there were moments in the early weeks that were hard. There were moments when I felt awkward, out of place and a little disconnected from my friends and family. But with every social situation I experienced not drinking, the more confidence I gained.

To keep myself motivated, I focussed on the benefits I was experiencing. Within just a few weeks of stopping drinking I noticed that my mornings were brighter. I woke up early naturally, ready to take on the day instead of dragging myself out of bed with a groggy head. I was sleeping better than I had in years, and that alone was enough to keep me going.

The clarity that I felt in the mornings was something I hadn't realised I was missing. It very quickly became one of the most rewarding aspects for me. I call them my miracle mornings, I wake at 6 at the first ring of my alarm, sometimes even a few minutes before it goes off. Then I treat myself to a stretch and a coffee while enjoying the sunrise and fresh air before the kids wake up.

On those mornings I would sit outside in my garden appreciating the quiet and I would often write down things I was feeling grateful for to start the day. I have incorporated this gratitude practice into my First 100 Days Sober Challenge as I feel it's so important for your mindset.

There were ups and downs in those first few weeks and I still wasn't sure if it was going to be a forever decision for me but I made sure to remind myself that these changes take time. I found that taking a moment to enjoy the progress and the journey really helped me.

Building New Habits

As I navigated through the first few months of not drinking, I knew that in order to succeed I had to fill the void that alcohol had left behind. Drinking had been a part of so many aspects of my life, whether it was unwinding after a stressful day at work or catching up with friends. I needed to find new ways to socialise that felt fulfilling and not restrictive.

One of the most helpful strategies that I found very early on was finding alternatives to the alcohol-based rituals I had created. In the evenings, when I had previously used a glass of wine to take the edge off a stressful day, I started a ritual of a short, gentle yoga routine. It wasn't about sweaty intense workouts but gentle movements, stretching my body and quieting my mind. I found that my home yoga sessions not only relaxed me physically but gave my mind a reset. Something I falsely believed alcohol had given me before.

Along with my yoga routine I started to replace my evening wine with a cup of herbal tea. Blends of camomile, lavender or valerian root, which were designed to help soothe and relax. This simple ritual became something I would really look forward to at the end of the day.

Reconnecting with nature was something else that helped me. I started going on more hikes and long walks. It was something that I had always enjoyed before but I had often neglected. Being outside in nature made me feel grounded and without the alcohol running through my body I truly appreciated the natural dopamine highs I got from reaching the top of a mountain trail, witnessing a sunrise over the ocean or swimming in natural water.

Being out in nature became almost like a therapy for me, it gave me space to reflect, to breathe and to reconnect with myself in a way I had not done for years. The more time I spent experiencing these highs of nature the less I missed the artificial highs I used to get from alcohol.

I rediscovered my love of reading. Without alcohol clouding my brain I was able to dive into books with a new level of focus. I read everything from fiction to self-help and personal development books, each one becoming an escape for me and a learning opportunity. I was absorbing the information like a sponge and found myself open to learning more and more about my health and happiness. Reading helped keep my mind busy and eager to learn, something alcohol had prevented in the past.

Creative and mindful colouring is something that I found a new joy in. I had always loved colouring as a child, and I've always been a creative person. Doing some colouring in the evenings is a great way to relieve stress and be mindful, and the colour combinations gave me a creative outlet that was easy and relaxing. I have added some colouring pages to the workbook at the end of this book to help you get through the First 100 Days Sober Challenge.

Without alcohol clouding my judgement I started to make more conscious decisions about what I was putting into my body. I became more attuned to how different foods made me feel, both physically and mentally. This wasn't about eating for weight loss, although that did happen naturally. It was about feeling nourished from the inside out.

Mealtimes became more enjoyable. I was spending more time cooking and enjoying being in the kitchen. In the past, after a glass of wine I would have looked for a quick and easy fix for dinner, sometimes reaching for salty snacks like crisps or cheese. I noticed how my cravings for these snack foods just disappeared once I stopped drinking and I began to truly enjoy the process of cooking and eating mindfully.

My appetite for late night snacking disappeared completely. I would often regret those salty snacks and wine in the evenings when I would wake up thirsty and dehydrated the next morning. Without alcohol triggering these cravings I simply wasn't eating them. I would go to bed without overindulging and wake up feeling great the next day.

One of the most notable changes was how much more I enjoyed my food. When I was drinking, meals out were often accompanied by a glass of wine, and I realised that alcohol had dulled my taste buds. Without it, food tasted better, fruits were sweeter, spices more vibrant and simple meals felt more satisfying. This wasn't always the case though. Some dining experiences went the opposite way. Without the glass of wine, I became more aware of poor food - it just wasn't enjoyable if it wasn't cooked well. I started to really embrace my own cooking.

By making healthier food choices, I was reinforcing the decision I had made to take better care of myself and my body. It felt like another way to honour and respect my body, listening to what it needed and responding with care and gratitude.

As a result of this I began to notice the effects in other areas of my life. I had more energy during my workouts, which in turn helped me sleep better. I was tired at bedtime and woke up fresh in the mornings.

However, socialising without alcohol required a bit more effort. The mummy drinking friendships had been built up with casual drinking most weeks and the nights out and birthday celebrations always involved alcohol. I had to get a little more creative by planning social gatherings that didn't revolve around alcohol.

Coffee dates became my go to way of socialising. These became even more enjoyable than drinking in bars for me. When we were all socialising over coffee I felt connected and present with my friends. There was something about the simplicity of a great cup of coffee and a meaningful conversation that felt so real.

Dancing is something that has always been important to me. I trained as a dancer from when I was little and feeling the music in my body is something I have always loved. In the past I had relied on alcohol to loosen me up in night clubs and on the dance floor. I felt like I needed that liquid courage to feel confident. But once I started going out sober I realised I loved dancing without having a drink. It was even more fun than before because I was fully present in the moment. I was solid on my feet, no wobbling or swaying. I wasn't embarrassing myself, I was having the best time, fully aware and completely myself without caring what others who were drunk on the dance floor thought about me.

Beyond the normal social situations, I started to make time for activities that were more in line with my new lifestyle. I would plan early morning sunrise hikes and brunches (minus the booze). Trips to the theatre to see shows, concerts and films at the cinema. These activities felt far more enriching than spending hours sitting in a noisy crowded bar. They left me feeling fulfilled rather than drained.

I was embracing my new found freedom of being able to leave an event whenever I wanted, without the pressure of staying out late drinking and keeping pace with those around me. This new way of socialising made me realise that I didn't need alcohol to have fun, to connect with friends or to enjoy life. It was eye opening.

Tools and Strategies: Staying on Track

These new habits I was building were essential to keep me away from alcohol, but there were also some tools and strategies I used to help me stay on track and be accountable.

One of the tools I found most useful at the beginning of my sobriety journey was tracking. I developed the Sobrezza tracking app to help me stay accountable with my sobriety. Each day I would log onto the app, make a pledge to myself about why I was doing this and I would read the daily motivational quotes to help me stay on track. Each day that I stayed alcohol free felt like a small win and seeing the days accumulating really helped my mindset.

Finding a community of sober-curious and sober women on Instagram really helped me as well. It was so motivating seeing other women's journeys and reaping the benefits of sobriety. I started to share my journey as well and loved the support I received. It felt great to know there were so many other people going through the same stages that I was.

Gratitude played a huge role in my sobriety. Every morning, I made a point of writing down three simple things that I was grateful for, whether they were milestones or small moments of joy. This simple practice helped my mind stay focussed on all the things I was gaining on my journey rather than on what I was "missing out" on by not drinking. It helped me to stay positive, even on days when challenges felt overwhelming. It's something that I found so helpful in my journey and I am so passionate about to this day that I wanted to share it in the workbook part of this book.

By building new habits, staying focussed, mindful and surrounding myself with a strong support system, I found that sobriety was not at all about deprivation. It was an opportunity for growth, connection and living life to the fullest. While the first few weeks had been challenging, they were also transformative. They taught me that I was capable of more than I had ever imagined and that life without alcohol was more colourful, fun and beautiful than I had ever believed possible.

Chapter 4

Discovering the Beauty of Life Sober

Mental Clarity and Personal Growth

The further I ventured into my journey of sobriety, the more I began to realise how I didn't need alcohol anymore. For years I had thought I needed that glass of wine to feel confident and fun. But the more socialising I did, the more nights out I experienced and people I met without alcohol, the clearer it became. I simply didn't need it.

After each interaction I had, I found myself more and more relaxed and confident than I had ever been while I was drinking. Alcohol had always blurred the edges of conversations, think slurred words, forgetting names and a lack of genuine connection.

Without alcohol I was more present. I could listen more deeply and respond more thoughtfully. Most importantly, I could remember every word of every conversation. There was no more foggy fumbling to remember what I had said the night before or wondering if I had come across in a way I hadn't intended.

One of the things that really surprised me was how my anxiety about socialising melted away within the first few minutes of a conversation. Those initial moments, where I might once have reached for a drink to ease myself in, no longer felt uncomfortable.

Once the conversation began flowing, I realised that I didn't need a glass of wine to make me feel confident. In fact, my confidence was more authentic, more genuine and I felt grounded knowing I could handle any social situation without the crutch of a drink in my hand. It was truly empowering.

Over time I began to really appreciate the ability to show up to social events as myself. There was no mask of alcohol to hide behind, no glass in my hand to blur the edges. Instead, I was present, engaged and connecting with people in a way I hadn't before. I learned that true confidence doesn't come from what we drink, it comes from deep within and feeling comfortable in our own skin.

Physical and Emotional Benefits

As I have mentioned in the previous chapter, a lot of the physical benefits of quitting alcohol started within just the first few weeks, but as time went on, they just kept getting better for me.

With my improved sleep and early morning routine solidly formed, my health improved in all areas. There were no more foggy days, instead every day I was waking up rejuvenated and ready to take on the day.

Along with better sleep came an increase in energy. I found myself smashing out workouts with a new lease of life. Hikes became easier and my body became stronger. Exercise became my new source of dopamine, leaving me with a sustainable high after workouts that made me feel alive.

Without alcohol in my body my immune system got a massive boost. I used to get sick quite often, colds, flu and general exhaustion, especially after nights of heavy drinking. But as I embraced a sober lifestyle, I noticed that I wasn't getting sick nearly as much.

My body felt stronger and more able to fight off infections. It made sense. My body was spending less time processing and getting rid of alcohol and more time working on the things I actually wanted it to be doing. Fighting off infections, keeping me strong and helping me rest and recover.

Another huge change I experienced was in my hormonal balance. Before quitting alcohol, my menstrual cycle was often irregular and unpredictable. Like many women, I thought it was normal - that erratic cycles and heavy periods should be something to live with. I put this down to stress or just how my body worked.

After cutting out alcohol my cycle began to regulate itself. This was an unexpected benefit but month after month my periods become more predictable and less painful. It was clear that alcohol had made a difference to my hormones.

Physically I was in the best shape of my life but emotionally I was thriving too. I was never really an anxious person but I felt like a weight had been lifted off me when I stopped drinking. I wasn't worrying about my children in the same way I had been before, I wasn't stressing about money or bills.

I wasn't waking up in the night worrying about work deadlines or life problems. I became more present in my life with my children. I was more engaged with my work, waking up motivated and excited to get into new projects. My productivity skyrocketed and 2023 became my highest earning year to date.

I felt grounded and at one with nature, whether it was walking along the beach feeling the sand between my toes or swimming in the sea, feeling the cool water on my body, I felt more connected to the world than ever. The simple pleasures, like feeling the sun on my face or the sound of the waves, became new sources of joy to me.

My Sober Experiences

40th Birthday Ibiza Girls Weekend

One of the milestones of my sober journey has to be celebrating my 40th birthday in Ibiza - completely sober. The Spanish island is notorious for wild parties, drugs and all-night drinking sessions and my birthday plans were well under way before I decided to start my sober journey.

I knew I still wanted to celebrate my birthday in Ibiza and the thought of spending my milestone birthday there without alcohol initially seemed unimaginable to both me and my friends. But as the day approached, I felt a new sense of excitement about experiencing the party island in a new and different way.

On the night of my birthday, we had arranged to go to an outdoor club with 80's music. I was dressed up and feeling great! So happy to be surrounded by the friends I loved. I let myself go with the rhythm of the music and fed off the crowd, the lights and the hot summer night air.

A few years back I never would have imagined I would be sober on a night out like this. But I felt amazing, the music flowed through my body, the beat syncing to my own energy. I danced the night away, enjoying every second. I was just living in the moment. At some point I closed my eyes and just felt the music pumping through my body. It was incredible.

I didn't have to worry about endless trips to the toilet because I was only drinking water, I went once and despite dancing my socks off all night my makeup still looked flawless. When I used to look in the mirror in night clubs my mascara would be round my eyes and I would look sweaty and drained. I still looked and felt fresh.

As the night grew to an end, I realised just how much energy I still had. I didn't want to go home and could have carried on dancing for another few hours. I was buzzing off the adrenaline. I felt so free, free to fully let loose and immerse myself in the moment without a drink in my hand.

The next morning, I woke up hangover free and ready to enjoy the beauty of the island. I was surrounded by the people that I love, I was glowing and there was nothing that could have made that weekend any better.

That evening we took a sunset boat trip and as I stood on the boat, feeling the gentle sway of the sea beneath me and the warmth of the evening sun, the beauty of the sunset brought a tear to my eye.

I was so present, so connected to the world and the people around me, I felt this overwhelming sense of gratitude and love. I savoured every single second of that weekend, my senses heightened by the absence of alcohol in my system. After that weekend I truly felt that I never had the need to drink again.

First Sober Family Holiday

Every Easter me and my children visit Lanzarote for a week to take a break from work and school. 2023 was the first time I went on this holiday without drinking alcohol. My days began early, as I woke up feeling refreshed each morning, hangover free of course.

I savoured breakfast with the kids, enjoying the fresh fruit and hot coffee. I would spend some time in the gym working out then go for a swim in the pool. While the children played throughout the day, I ate up the books I was reading, getting lost in them and truly relaxing for the first time in ages.

I watched other parents at the pool drinking cocktails and saw their energy fade throughout the day, often woozy and sunburnt by dinner time. I didn't have any desire or urge to drink on that holiday. I felt present and fully there to share every moment with my family, from their laughter in the pool to our evening walks along the beach.

When we got back home, I felt truly energised from the break away and ready to get back to work. The complete opposite from what you hear from many parents after a family holiday, complaining that they need another holiday when they get home.

Finding Joy in Everyday Life

One of the greatest gifts I have experienced since quitting alcohol is the ability to rediscover the simple pleasures in life. Sunrises and sunsets have taken on a new meaning for me, each one feels like a reminder of a new fresh start or the significance and peace of the end of a day.

Something about that new opportunity each morning is really meaningful for me. We often aren't present enough to appreciate this. I have learned to absorb moments like this, to enjoy the quiet and peaceful parts of life that often get overlooked while we are distracted with the chaos that normally surrounds us.

For me gratitude has become a daily practice. Each morning, I take a few minutes to reflect on the things I am grateful for at this moment in my life. It can be the smallest of things, but doing this gives me focus and peace. Even on the worst days, I can always find something to be grateful for. Finding this gratitude within has really helped me on my journey and I encourage you to include this daily practice in your own sobriety journey.

Sobriety has brought me a new level of confidence within my own skin. For years I have suffered with body issues and I finally feel like I have reached a moment in my life where I am comfortable with how I look and feel.

I have grown to appreciate my body for how it works, what it can do rather than how it looks. I feel stronger, healthier and more in tune with myself than ever before.

How Sobriety Deepened My Relationships

Another of the changes I have experienced through sobriety has been in my relationships. Without the layer of fog from alcohol I have been able to connect on a different level with friends, family and loved ones. Conversations are rich, engaging and most importantly, memorable.

One thing I am so grateful for is the relationship with my mum which, while already strong, has only got stronger since I have quit drinking. While at the beginning she was a bit unsure of my decision and vowed she would never be able to quit drinking, she has slowly been influenced by my journey and she too has decided to stop drinking.

We have bonded over our shared journey and support each other through the ups and downs of navigating the social landscape without alcohol. We have definitely grown closer as a result.

Many of my friends have also been inspired by my journey, with several of them joining me for a Dry January this year, and some have reduced their drinking habits. The conversations we now have are motivating, about life, goals and personal growth, rather than funny drunk stories or where we are going for the next drink. I feel more connected to my closest friends and I value the honesty and trust that has come from these relationships.

In the end, quitting drinking has given me so much more than I ever expected. It has allowed me to live a life that is bright, joyful and full of focus and meaning. The beauty of life that was once dulled by the haze of booze is now vibrant and breath taking. And for that I am forever grateful.

Chapter 5

Navigating Social Situations – Socially Sober Hacks

Discovering how to socialise sober with confidence and self-belief was one of the most game changing moments for me. When I began my journey, I realised that drinking was woven into the fabric of so many social interactions.

Events and meet ups were often accompanied by alcohol. But over time I learned how to navigate these situations without alcohol and enjoy them! I have put together this chapter to help you to confidently do the same, including some of my own socially sober hacks that I use when socialising sober.

Building a Supportive Social Network

When I first made the decision to stop drinking alcohol, one of my biggest fears was how my friendship circle might change. Would I lose friends over my decision? Would I feel isolated? Would I just stop going out, doomed to stay in and be lonely forever? What would my friends think when I said I wasn't going to be drinking? Would they think I was boring and stop inviting me out? I was honest with my friends and as we all grew to be comfortable with my choices, I realised that our relationships would naturally grow too.

One of the best ways that I have found to maintain my close network of friends is to find activities that don't always revolve around alcohol. A lot of my friends enjoy fitness and spending time outdoors so it was easy for me to suggest things like hiking or classes at the gym.

I also participated in other activities that were not focussed on drinking, like forming a book club or movie and game nights, which were so much fun. A lot of my friends were open to trying sober activities and respected my decision. I hosted some dinner parties, birthday parties and brunches without alcohol and no one missed the drinking aspect at all.

Finding these new environments and activities is crucial in your journey to sobriety. If you are constantly surrounded by people who drink heavily or are always sitting in bars you may find it harder to stay strong in your decision. Not to mention when you are the only one not drinking people can become loud and annoying, and you may even wonder what you had in common with them other than drinking in the first place.

I switched out my drinking in bars with day time coffee dates with friends. No one missed the alcohol and the conversations became more meaningful and memorable. My existing friendships deepened and I felt more fulfilled.

Planning for Success

Early on in my journey I realised that spontaneity could sometimes lead to temptation so planning ahead was key. Preparing yourself for a night out or a social event where you know alcohol will be served is essential. Setting clear intentions for the night and having a plan in place really helps.

First I like to decide what I am going to drink before I even leave the house. Whether it is sparkling water, a mocktail or another type of non-alcoholic drink, knowing that the venue I am going to will serve these drinks makes me feel prepared and confident.

I have found that having a drink in my hand when socialising, even if it is non-alcoholic, eases my awkwardness and helps me blend in at events where others are drinking. If I am invited to someone's house I often take a bottle of my homemade kombucha, or sparkling water or even some herbal tea bags. This way I always know I have my preferred drink and I won't feel left out.

Another essential tip is to have an exit plan. I'm not saying you always have to leave early, but having a way out of a situation that may feel uncomfortable or triggering is important. One thing I tend to do is take my car with me, this way I can leave when I am ready. If I am driving other people, I like to make sure I say I will be leaving at a certain time and they can get a taxi if they want to stay later. This means I am always in control of when I leave.

Setting clear intentions before the night is a great way to stay on track. I like to remind myself of my personal reasons for choosing sobriety and how great I will feel in the morning when I wake up without a hangover. Knowing I will wake up clear-headed and ready for a bright day ahead of me, helps to keep me motivated to stick to my decision.

Sober Activity Ideas

Living a sober life absolutely doesn't mean that your social life has to be boring. In fact, it can open up doors to many new experiences and activities that don't involve drinking. Here are my top 10 ideas to try when socialising sober:

1. Hiking or nature walks.

A perfect opportunity to reconnect with nature. These can be done solo or with friends. Giving you time for personal reflection or meaningful conversation and catching up. Taking time to explore new places makes each new location a new adventure.

2. Beach days or picnics in the park.

Another great way to spend time outdoors. Pack some of your favourite non-alcoholic drinks and snacks. Spend time swimming in the sea, playing games or simply relaxing with a good book. Fresh air and sunshine help to give you an energy and spirit boost.

3. Fitness classes or group workouts.

Joining a fitness class or working out with a group can be a great way to stay healthy and connect with others who prioritise health. Spinning, cross fit or dance and cardio classes are a few examples where the shared focus is fitness and can give you an uplifting positive boost.

4. Yoga retreats or wellness weekends.

Weekends away or retreats can offer a break from the stress of everyday life. These retreats often focus on mindfulness, clean eating and physical movement, leaving you feeling refreshed, centred and empowered to continue your sober journey.

5. Cooking classes and potluck dinner parties.

Learning new cooking skills is always fun, especially the preparing and tasting of delicious food. Potluck dinner parties where everyone prepares and brings a dish are a cosy way to share food together, where the focus is on connection rather than drinking.

6. Attending live theatre or concerts.

Attending live concerts and theatres is always a thrilling experience. Enjoying live performances and feeling the energy of the crowd. You will be amazed at the buzz you can get when you immerse yourself in the event without a drink.

7. Going to the cinema or hosting movie nights.

Whether it's going to the cinema or hosting a cosy film night at home, movies are a great way to unwind and immerse yourself in another world for a few hours.

8. Exploring new coffee shops or tea houses.

A great place to meet up with friends or enjoy a solo trip. I am always interested in trying new cafes, testing their offerings and enjoying some meaningful conversations and catch ups with friends.

9. Hosting game nights with friends.

Game nights are a super fun way to spend time with friends. Board games, card games and even video games can provide hours of entertainment and joy. It’s an easy way to spend time bonding, laughing and enjoying each other’s company.

10. Joining a book club or starting your own.

A book club can be a great way to combine socialising and intellectual stimulation. Meeting up regularly to discuss the book helps you connect with others but also keeps your mind engaged and challenged.

These activities not only keep you connected with others, but they also allow you to create meaningful memories that aren’t always linked to drinking.

Socially Sober Hacks

When navigating social situations sober it's great to have a little collection of hacks to go to - especially when you are just at the beginning of your journey. Here are 10 of my top hacks to help you manage any social situation.

1. Hold a non-alcoholic drink in your hand so no one offers you one.

By keeping a drink in your hand, you avoid being offered another drink. People often assume you are set if you have a drink in your hand, and aren't really bothered what you are drinking. Helping you to blend in without having to explain your choice.

2. Prepare a polite but firm response when someone asks why you're not drinking.

Be ready to answer with a simple, clear response. I have included a few of my conversation hacks in the next section.

3. Bring your own non-alcoholic beverages to events.

By bringing your favourite drink to a social event you always have an option with you that you enjoy. My personal favourite is a bottle of my homemade kombucha.

4. Leave early if the vibe feels too centred on drinking.

If you find yourself getting uncomfortable or overwhelmed by a heavy drinking environment, leaving early can help you avoid temptation.

5. Drive yourself to the event so you can leave whenever you need to.

This is one hack I often rely on. It gives you the flexibility to leave whenever you want to. You won't be relying on anyone else to get you home at the end of the night.

6. Suggest activities that don't revolve around alcohol.

Redirect your social plans by suggesting alternative activities, whether it's a hike in nature, a fitness class or a day time coffee meet. This helps to support your journey and also helps to introduce others to enjoyable alcohol-free socialising.

7. Focus on the positive benefits of sobriety when tempted.

When faced with temptation, remind yourself of how great you feel, whether it's better sleep, clarity or weight loss. Focussing on the positives helps you to stick to your commitment to not drink.

8. Surround yourself with friends who support your choice.

Having a good network of positive, understanding friends will make it easier for you to maintain sobriety. Remove any toxic friends who don't support you in your journey. If they cannot respect your decision, they are not your friends.

9. Be confident in your choice, knowing you're doing what's best for you.

Trust yourself! You know your body best and knowing that you feel great not drinking is a decision you can feel confident making.

10. Visualise how great you'll feel the next morning without a hangover.

This is one hack that never gets old for me. Knowing that at the end of the night I will take off my makeup, do my skincare routine, get a great night's sleep and wake up feeling fresh in the morning is a great motivator to stay alcohol free.

At the end of the day, remember that most people don't care what you're drinking - they're more focused on themselves.

Conversation Hacks

When you are socialising without alcohol it is almost inevitable that someone will ask you why you are not having an alcoholic drink. Here are 20 of my favourite conversation hacks to help you respond with confidence.

1. "I'm on a health kick right now!"
2. "I feel so much better when I don't drink."
3. "I'm driving tonight."
4. "I'm just taking a break from alcohol."
5. "I've got an early start tomorrow."
6. "I'm focusing on fitness and don't want to mess with my progress."
7. "I'm trying out new non-alcoholic drinks!"
8. "I realised I enjoy myself more without it."
9. "I don't really like the taste of alcohol anymore."
10. "I'm just not feeling it tonight."
11. "I'm giving myself a little challenge to go alcohol-free."
12. "I'm doing a cleanse right now."
13. "I'm in the middle of a sober streak and loving it."
14. "I feel more present without alcohol."
15. "I have a big workout planned for tomorrow."
16. "I'm enjoying how clear-headed I feel these days."
17. "I find I'm more fun without alcohol!"
18. "I'm sticking to sparkling water tonight."
19. "I just feel so much better without it."
20. "I'm loving the sober life!"

These responses help to keep the conversation light and don't make sobriety out to be a big deal. They also help to shift the conversation away from drinking and onto more meaningful conversations.

I hope you will incorporate some of these tips, strategies and hacks into your next sober social event. Remember you can continue to enjoy socialising without alcohol. It doesn't mean you are missing out, it just means you are embracing every moment of life with a clear mind and body.

Chapter 6
Your First 100 Days Sober Challenge

My Challenge to you!

Now that you have read my story and armed yourself with the hacks and tips I use in my sobriety, I challenge you to join me with my First 100 Days Sober Challenge. I want you to also experience the highs of life and freedom and confidence to socialise without alcohol. I have put together this challenge along with a workbook to track your progress and journey along the way.

Introduction to the 100-Day Challenge

For me the 100-day milestone marked a turning point in my journey. The challenge was about more than just the decision to stop drinking. It was a chance to fully experience the beauty of life without alcohol. Thanks to 100 days of no drinking, my eyes were opened and I learned to embrace the highs and lows, discovering a new authentic side of myself and reaping all the benefits that came with it. And I know you will too.

The concept of embarking on a 100-day sober challenge was a powerful concept that I felt truly passionate about including in this book. While many people commit to a Dry January or a 30-day detox challenge, the decision to extend this to 100 days is about more than just adding in the extra time. 100 days gives enough time and space to go beyond the surface of habit building and gives you an opportunity to really experience life without alcohol.

Why 100 days?

As you will have learned from my story, initially I would often commit to 30-day alcohol-free challenges—Dry January, Whole 30, or personal detoxes. But while I felt great after a month, I would soon fall back into old patterns. I found that the longer I kept off drinking alcohol, the more profound my personal growth became. I had more opportunities to get out into the world and socialise, go on holiday or a weekend away and more opportunities to interact in situations where alcohol was present.

These additional days gave me a chance to create more lasting habits, shift my mindset and start appreciating the beauty of the world without the haze of alcohol over it. While 30 days may be enough for the body to detox, 100 days will transform your mind, habits and daily routines.

You will see how far you can go, crossing over boundaries and discovering your true self. For me it has become a journey of self-empowerment and euphoria and I want to offer the same challenge to you.

Celebrating Milestones Along the Way

Your First 100 Days Sober Challenge can feel intimidating at first but I want to break it down into manageable milestones. I found this helpful myself and want you to celebrate each one and be proud of how far you have come. Each milestone gives you an opportunity to reflect on the progress you have made and rejoice in your journey so far.

Days 1-30: The Dawn Phase

The first 30 days of the challenge are all about detoxing. Your body will be adjusting slowly to life without alcohol, in this phase your cravings for alcohol might be at their strongest. This phase is a great time to focus on self-care and building up habits and new routines. Journaling can be helpful as well as drinking plenty of water. Get outside during this time, take walks, get grounded and breathe.

Spend some time joining a sober community for motivation and support. There are some great ones on Instagram as well as Facebook. If you have one local to you that would be great or team up with a sober support buddy.

Tracking your progress can be useful during this phase, you can appreciate every day you make it through. Appreciate the progress you are making. I am so proud of you.

Days 31-60: The Blossoming Sunrise Phase

By day 30, your body has started to adjust. You might start noticing some amazing physical benefits at this point. You may have lost some weight, your skin may be looking brighter, your sleep will have improved and your energy levels may be up. Your mind will be clear and your cravings for alcohol may feel reduced by this point.

Use this time to push yourself out of your comfort zone. Attend some social events where you know alcohol will be present. Use the Socially Sober Hacks from the previous chapter to make these events flow smoothly. It's also a great time to explore some new hobbies. Now that your mind is clear and focussed it's the perfect time to try something new.

Make sure you celebrate your wins, take a look back at how far you have come. Take note of all the small changes you are experiencing as these will help to keep you motivated.

Days 61-90: The Radiance Phase

At this stage the benefits of sobriety are becoming clearer in your mind, the temptations are easier to manage. You will feel so empowered by the progress you have made. You will feel confident going out and managing social situations alcohol free. Continue to challenge yourself by socialising more.

Consider hosting a sober event like a dinner party or a brunch and create some delicious food and mocktails for your guests. Introduce them to your beautiful sober world.

By this point you have proven to yourself that you can socialise easily without alcohol and that life is radiant and beautiful without it. You will be feeling the best you have felt in a long time.

Days 91-100: The Golden Horizon Phase

The last stretch of the challenge is a point of celebration! Look at how far you have come! Both physically and mentally. At this point you have likely redefined what fun looks like when socialising and you have a brand new perspective of life.

Celebrating this milestone can involve planning an event or treating yourself to something special. Most importantly, take time to look back on how far you have come. You have achieved a huge personal transformation and I am so proud of you.

As you progress through each phase, I encourage you to use this book as a workbook. Track your daily progress, note how you're feeling and celebrate every milestone along the way. This self-reflection will help you see your growth and reinforce your motivation to keep going.

Practical Tips for Success

A big part of the success of your First 100 Days Sober Challenge comes from planning ahead. Having the right tools and strategies in place can help you succeed in managing triggers and temptations. Here are some practical tips that have helped me and I hope they will help you too.

1. Daily reflections and journaling.

I journaled every day when I started my sobriety journey. It allowed me to express my feelings, emotions and vent any frustrations. It was also a great way to look back when I was having a hard day to see how far I had come. Reflection helps you to gain clarity on your own journey and process how you feel without alcohol.

In the workbook at the end of the book there is space each day to fill out how you are feeling, set your daily intention and record what you are grateful for. Especially in the beginning, finding ways to be grateful along your journey can be very helpful.

2. Manage cravings with new rituals.

In the beginning, especially in the first phase, cravings can be strong and feel overwhelming. If you find it helpful, replace these cravings with healthier alternatives ones that serve you better.

For example, one of the rituals I use in the evenings is to brew some herbal tea, complete my yoga practice and journal. This helps my mind and body feel at peace and calm.

I have also included some mindful colouring practices for each milestone of your journey. You can enjoy these as a relaxing activity.

3. Set clear goals and celebrate every success.

Setting goals for each milestone of the challenge can help you stay on track. If it's appropriate, set yourself goals for each phase. For example, "attend at least 1 social event per week" or "enjoy 4 hangover free Sundays this month."

Plan small treats and rewards for yourself after completing milestones, whether it's a new book, a special meal out with your partner or a spa weekend. Rewarding yourself is important.

4. Stay connected.

Surround yourself with a positive community. Online communities like Instagram and Facebook can help you to connect with others on the same path and cheer each other on. Follow me at The.Sober.Goddess and tag me in your milestone progress, I would love to see how you are getting on!

Find friends who understand your journey and consider recruiting a sober buddy to go on this journey with.

5. Visualise success.

Whenever you feel tempted to break the challenge, visualise how amazing you will feel when you reach 100 days hangover free. Picture yourself at your very best, thriving in sobriety and reaping all the benefits that go along with it. This visualisation exercise is super powerful and can really help override moments of doubt.

6. Use the Sobrezza app.

Tracking your progress every day can make the challenge feel more structured. I created the Sobrezza app to track each sober day and celebrate milestones along the way. You can download it for free from the App store. It offers daily motivation along your journey and helps you measure your progress.

A Path to Long-Lasting Change

I designed your First 100 Days Sober Challenge to go beyond just quitting alcohol. It is about redesigning your life and thriving without it. It's an opportunity to experience life to its fullest when you are present, healthy and committed to your wellbeing.

It may seem difficult at first but with each day your confidence and self-belief will grow and soon you will realise that you don't need alcohol to enjoy life or to have fun and be social.

The extra time that you have dedicated to this challenge allows your mindset to shift and for you to develop deep long-lasting habits. You will likely find new hobbies, develop deeper relationships, see amazing benefits in your health, sleep, and stress levels and uncover a joy to life that was dulled by drinking.

What if I slip up?

Please remember, it's ok if you don't make it to the 100 days on your first try. This challenge is about progress, not perfection. If you slip up, don't be hard on yourself!

Whether you have managed 30 days or even just a week, celebrate this as a victory and a testament to your strength. Instead of viewing this as a setback, consider it a part of a larger journey.

Many people can successfully manage moderate drinking after completing a period of sobriety so if you do choose to enjoy an occasional drink after the challenge you will have a much more mindful approach than before and you may find you never return to the same drinking habits you had previously.

Completing the First 100 Days Sober Challenge may just be the beginning of a new chapter in your life. One where you no longer depend on alcohol to feel good, but instead rely on the confidence, clarity and joy that comes from within.

Final Thoughts

Reflecting on Your Journey

As you stand here at the end of this book, take a moment to reflect on how far you have come. Whether you have completed a 30-day challenge, or have chosen to take on my First 100 Days Sober Challenge, or even if you are just considering cutting down on your intake of alcohol, it's important to recognise the incredible growth you have experienced since you first decided to pick up this book.

What started as a sober curious thought to commit to a step away from alcohol has hopefully evolved into something much more powerful, a journey of self-discovery, transformation and empowerment.

From the start of your own sober journey you have undergone some amazing changes, not only physically and mentally but also emotionally. Remember those early days when it seemed impossible to imagine going to a social event without a glass of wine in your hand? Or to even picture yourself winding down from a hard day without that drink before bed?

You have learned that it is not only possible but it's also incredibly rewarding. Your body has thanked you for giving it time to heal. You may have noticed more restful sleep, weight loss, clear skin and an energy boost. These changes are just the beginning.

You may be feeling a clarity that you haven't felt for years. That fog that had been hazing over you, affecting your decision making, productivity and relationships has now lifted. You are sharper, more focussed and able to experience joy in new ways.

Without alcohol dulling your emotions you are able to appreciate a new awareness of how you are feeling, both the good and the difficult moments. You have become better at facing challenges head on, being honest with yourself instead of reaching for a drink to numb the emotions.

You may have noticed changes in your relationships too. Perhaps this journey has allowed you to connect with people in unexpected ways and allowed connections to deepen, or break apart. Without the haze of alcohol, conversations become more meaningful, laughter is more genuine and moments shared with loved ones are secured in your memory.

Sobriety has brought you close to the people who matter most to you and has given you the tools to build stronger, healthier, more genuine relationships in the future that don't revolve around getting drunk.

Your journey, whether this is just the beginning or you are in it for the long run, is a true testament to your strength, resilience and self-belief. You can be proud of yourself that you are committing to a better and more fulfilling life. Be sure to take a minute to look back, acknowledge the milestones, the moments of struggle and celebrate all the growth you have achieved. The path is not always easy or straightforward but I guarantee it is one of the most worthwhile journeys you will ever take.

Next Steps

Now that you have finished reading this book and perhaps you have completed your First 100 Days Sober Challenge, what is next for you? The end of the challenge or a milestone doesn't mean the end of your journey - it's simply a new beginning.

You have set down the groundwork for long term change, and the next phase is about continuing to build on the habits and insights that you have gained.

If you have completed the First 100 Days Sober Challenge you will be wondering whether to extend your sobriety even further. For many, 100 days is enough to provide a glimpse of what life can be like without alcohol but it's also just the start.

Consider exploring long term sobriety and the huge number of benefits that come with it. By now you have experienced how much more energy, focus and joy you can have in everyday life. Why not continue to see how far this journey can take you?

Beyond alcohol, think about all of the new habits, routines and experiences you have cultivated during this journey. Whether it's morning routines, evening meditation, creative passions or just spending more time with the people you love. These experiences and positive changes are important to appreciate moving forward. You will want to continue nurturing these habits, supporting your physical, mental and emotional health.

Your journey doesn't end in 100 days. It's an ongoing process of growth, learning and transformation. Take each and every day as it comes, continue setting goals and remember that sobriety is a commitment to your health, happiness and wellbeing. You have proven that you have the strength to take on this challenge. There is no limit to what you can achieve.

Here's to your continued success and the next chapter of your sober, joy filled life. Keep going, stay strong and remember that you are capable of incredible things. I am so proud of how far you have come and can't wait to see where the rest of your journey takes you.

Additional Resources

Embarking on a sober journey is a powerful, life-changing experience, and staying connected with resources, tools and supportive communities can help maintain your progress. This resources section offers a variety of books, podcasts, documentaries, online communities and apps that can guide and inspire you along the way.

Books, Podcasts, and Documentaries on Sobriety

1. Books:

- *This Naked Mind* by Annie Grace
- A ground breaking approach to understanding the science behind alcohol and how to regain control over your relationship with it.
- *Quit Like a Woman* by Holly Whitaker
- A radical feminist approach to addiction and sobriety that challenges conventional recovery methods.
- *The Unexpected Joy of Being Sober* by Catherine Gray
- Gray shares her personal journey to sobriety with humour, wisdom and hope, showing how life without alcohol is full of unexpected joys.
- *We Are the Luckiest: The Surprising Magic of a Sober Life* by Laura McKowen
- A memoir of recovery that explores the transformation and healing that come with choosing sobriety.

2. Podcasts:

- **The Sober Curious Podcast:** Hosted by Ruby Warrington, this podcast delves into the cultural norms around drinking and encourages listeners to rethink their relationship with alcohol.
- **Recovery Elevator:** A podcast aimed at helping listeners who want to quit drinking and live a more fulfilling life without alcohol.
- **Soberful:** Veronica Valli and Chip Somers bring over 50 years of experience in sobriety to their discussions about living alcohol-free.
- **The Bubble Hour:** Hosted by Jean McCarthy, this podcast features stories of sobriety and recovery,

sharing insights, resources and strategies for living alcohol-free.

3. Documentaries:

- **"The Anonymous People":** A feature-length documentary that focuses on the 23.5 million Americans living in long-term recovery from addiction, aiming to change the conversation about recovery and destigmatise addiction.
- **"A Royal Hangover":** This documentary takes a critical look at the relationship between alcohol and British culture, exploring the effects of binge drinking and alcoholism.
- **"My Name Was Bette: The Life and Death of an Alcoholic":** A powerful documentary that tells the tragic story of Bette, a woman whose life was destroyed by alcoholism.
- **"Sober House":** A reality TV series following celebrities through rehab and recovery, offering an intimate look at the struggle to stay sober.

Online Communities and Support Groups

Finding support from others who are on the same journey can make a significant difference in your sobriety experience. Here are some online communities and support groups where you can find connection, guidance and encouragement:

1. **Instagram:**
    - **@The.Sober.Goddess**: A popular Instagram account offering inspiration, support and community for women choosing sobriety. Follow for daily posts, motivational quotes and connection with others embracing a sober lifestyle.
2. **Online Forums and Communities:**
    - **Soberistas:** A worldwide online community for women who want to quit drinking and live a healthier life. With articles, discussions and personal stories, this community provides support 24/7.
    - **Reddit: /r/StopDrinking:** A subreddit dedicated to people who are quitting drinking or already living alcohol-free. This is a vibrant community where members share their experiences, ask questions and support one another.
    - **Sober Recovery:** An online forum offering resources, discussions and personal stories for people in recovery. Members share experiences, advice and encouragement.
    - **Tempest Sobriety School:** An online platform offering coaching, resources and a supportive community for those looking to quit drinking or reduce their alcohol consumption.
    - **SMART Recovery:** A science-based, self-help program that provides free mutual support meetings

for people seeking independence from addictive behaviours.

3. **Local Meetups and In-Person Groups:**
   - **Alcoholics Anonymous (AA):** A global fellowship of people who share their experiences to help each other recover from alcoholism. Meetings are held worldwide and provide a safe space for those seeking sobriety.
   - **Women for Sobriety:** A self-help program for women focusing on positivity, emotional growth and self-respect. It offers online and in-person support groups.
   - **Celebrate Recovery:** A Christian-based 12-step program that helps individuals struggling with addiction, with groups located worldwide.
   - **Meetup: Sober Events:** Check local Meetup listings for sober social events and gatherings in your area. Activities may range from hikes and fitness classes to game nights and book clubs, all with a focus on building connections without alcohol.

Tools for Sobriety

Staying on track and managing your sobriety day by day is easier with the right tools. Here are some recommended apps and resources that offer tracking, mindfulness and community support:

1. Sobriety Tracking Apps:

- **Sobrezza App:** This free app offers daily motivation and a simple tracking tool for those looking to stay alcohol-free. With features like progress milestones and encouraging messages, it helps keep you on track and connected.
- **Sober Time:** Another tracking app that allows you to monitor your sobriety and provides motivational quotes, progress charts and reminders of the benefits of living alcohol-free.

2. Mindfulness and Meditation Apps:

- **Headspace:** A leading mindfulness app that offers guided meditations to help manage stress, cravings and emotional well-being. Meditation can be a powerful tool in supporting your sobriety journey.
- **Calm:** Similar to Headspace, Calm provides guided meditations, sleep stories and breathing exercises to help reduce stress and promote mindfulness.

3. Additional Resources for Support:

- **Sober Grid:** A social networking app specifically designed for people in recovery, Sober Grid connects you with a global sober community. You can chat with others, share your experiences and even find sober friends nearby.

- **Meetup: Sober Events:** Use Meetup to find sober social activities in your area, such as book clubs, yoga classes, fitness meetups or creative workshops.
- **AA Big Book App:** A digital version of the Alcoholics Anonymous Big Book, offering easy access to the program's core text, making it easier to read or reference on the go.

By incorporating these resources into your journey, you'll have a wide range of tools and support systems at your disposal to help you maintain and thrive in your sobriety. Whether it's through podcasts that uplift you, books that inspire you or apps that keep you accountable, these tools can serve as powerful companions along your path.

Remember, you are not alone on this journey, and the support of a community - whether online, in-person or through media - can make all the difference.

First 100 Sober Days Challenge Workbook

The Dawn Phase (Days 1-30)

What does sobriety mean to me?
Reflect on your feelings and thoughts about starting this journey. How do you envision your life without alcohol?

What challenges do I anticipate during this detox phase?
Identify potential triggers or situations that might tempt you to drink. How do you plan to cope with them?

What self-care activities can I incorporate into my daily routine?
List at least three activities (e.g., yoga, meditation, journaling) that can support you in this phase and help you feel more grounded.

The Dawn Phase (Days 1-30)

What are my goals for this challenge?
Define your main goals for the 100-day sobriety challenge. What do you hope to achieve during the first 30 days, whether physically, emotionally, or mentally?

What positive changes do I hope to see by the end of the detox phase?
Envision how you want to feel after completing these 30 days. What improvements do you hope to notice in your energy, mood, health or daily life?

How will I celebrate my progress after 30 days?
Plan a meaningful, non-alcoholic way to celebrate reaching the 30-day mark. How will you reward yourself for your hard work and dedication?

Day 1: Reflection

Today I am grateful for these three things...

1. ____________________
2. ____________________
3. ____________________

Date:

Sober Check in:

What is my intention for today?

____

____

How am I feeling right now?

____

____

Day 2: Reflection

Today I am grateful for these three things...

1. ____________________
2. ____________________
3. ____________________

Date:

Sober Check in:

What is my intention for today?

____

____

How am I feeling right now?

____

____

1DAY

Day 3: Reflection

Today I am grateful for these three things...

1. ______________________
2. ______________________
3. ______________________

Date:

Sober Check in:

What is my intention for today?

____

____

How am I feeling right now?

____

____

Day 4: Reflection

Today I am grateful for these three things...

1. ______________________
2. ______________________
3. ______________________

Date:

Sober Check in:

What is my intention for today?

____

____

How am I feeling right now?

____

____

Day 5: Reflection

Today I am grateful for these three things...

Date:

1. ______

2. ______

3. ______

Sober Check in:

What is my intention for today?

______

______

How am I feeling right now?

______

______

Day 6: Reflection

Today I am grateful for these three things...

Date:

1. ______

2. ______

3. ______

Sober Check in:

What is my intention for today?

______

______

How am I feeling right now?

______

______

Day 7: Reflection

Today I am grateful for these three things...

1. ______________________________
2. ______________________________
3. ______________________________

Date:

Sober Check in:

What is my intention for today?

How am I feeling right now?

Day 8: Reflection

Today I am grateful for these three things...

1. ______________________________
2. ______________________________
3. ______________________________

Date:

Sober Check in:

What is my intention for today?

How am I feeling right now?

1
WEEK

Day 9: Reflection

Today I am grateful for these three things...

Date:

1. ______________________________

2. ______________________________

Sober Check in:

3. ______________________________

What is my intention for today?

____

____

How am I feeling right now?

____

____

Day 10: Reflection

Today I am grateful for these three things...

Date:

1. ______________________________

2. ______________________________

Sober Check in:

3. ______________________________

What is my intention for today?

____

____

How am I feeling right now?

____

____

10 DAYS

Day 11: Reflection

Today I am grateful for these three things...

1. ______________________________
2. ______________________________
3. ______________________________

Date:

Sober Check in:

What is my intention for today?

____

____

How am I feeling right now?

____

____

Day 12: Reflection

Today I am grateful for these three things...

1. ______________________________
2. ______________________________
3. ______________________________

Date:

Sober Check in:

What is my intention for today?

____

____

How am I feeling right now?

____

____

Day 13: Reflection

Today I am grateful for these three things...

1. ____________________
2. ____________________
3. ____________________

Date:

Sober Check in:

What is my intention for today?

How am I feeling right now?

Day 14: Reflection

Today I am grateful for these three things...

1. ____________________
2. ____________________
3. ____________________

Date:

Sober Check in:

What is my intention for today?

How am I feeling right now?

Day 15: Reflection

Today I am grateful for these three things...

Date:

1. ______

2. ______

3. ______

Sober Check in:

What is my intention for today?

______

______

How am I feeling right now?

______

______

Day 16: Reflection

Today I am grateful for these three things...

Date:

1. ______

2. ______

3. ______

Sober Check in:

What is my intention for today?

______

______

How am I feeling right now?

______

______

Day 17: Reflection

Today I am grateful for these three things...

1. ____________________
2. ____________________
3. ____________________

Date:

Sober Check in:

What is my intention for today?

How am I feeling right now?

Day 18: Reflection

Today I am grateful for these three things...

1. ____________________
2. ____________________
3. ____________________

Date:

Sober Check in:

What is my intention for today?

How am I feeling right now?

Day 19: Reflection

Today I am grateful for these three things ..

1. ______________________
2. ______________________
3. ______________________

Date:

Sober Check in:

What is my intention for today?

____

____

How am I feeling right now?

____

____

Day 20: Reflection

Today I am grateful for these three things...

1. ______________________
2. ______________________
3. ______________________

Date:

Sober Check in:

What is my intention for today?

____

____

How am I feeling right now?

____

____

20
DAYS

Day 21: Reflection

Today I am grateful for these three things...

1. ______________________________
2. ______________________________
3. ______________________________

Date:

Sober Check in:

What is my intention for today?

____

____

How am I feeling right now?

____

____

Day 22: Reflection

Today I am grateful for these three things...

1. ______________________________
2. ______________________________
3. ______________________________

Date:

Sober Check in:

What is my intention for today?

____

____

How am I feeling right now?

____

____

Day 23: Reflection

Today I am grateful for these three things...

1. ______________________________
2. ______________________________
3. ______________________________

Date:

Sober Check in:

What is my intention for today?

How am I feeling right now?

Day 24: Reflection

Today I am grateful for these three things...

1. ______________________________
2. ______________________________
3. ______________________________

Date:

Sober Check in:

What is my intention for today?

How am I feeling right now?

Day 25: Reflection

Today I am grateful for these three things ..

1. ________________________
2. ________________________
3. ________________________

Date:

Sober Check in:

What is my intention for today?

How am I feeling right now?

Day 26: Reflection

Today I am grateful for these three things...

1. ________________________
2. ________________________
3. ________________________

Date:

Sober Check in:

What is my intention for today?

How am I feeling right now?

Day 27: Reflection

Today I am grateful for these three things...

1. ______________________
2. ______________________
3. ______________________

Date:

Sober Check in:

What is my intention for today?

____

____

How am I feeling right now?

____

____

Day 28: Reflection

Today I am grateful for these three things...

1. ______________________
2. ______________________
3. ______________________

Date:

Sober Check in:

What is my intention for today?

____

____

How am I feeling right now?

____

____

Day 29: Reflection

Today I am grateful for these three things...

1. ____________________
2. ____________________
3. ____________________

Date:

Sober Check in:

What is my intention for today?

____

____

How am I feeling right now?

____

____

Day 30: Reflection

Today I am grateful for these three things...

1. ____________________
2. ____________________
3. ____________________

Date:

Sober Check in:

What is my intention for today?

____

____

How am I feeling right now?

____

____

30 DAYS

The Blossoming Sunrise Phase (Days 31-60)

How have I noticed my mood or energy levels changing since starting this challenge?
Describe any positive shifts in your emotional state, energy or overall wellbeing.

What new activities have I discovered or want to explore?
List at least three new hobbies or interests you've tried or wish to try that don't involve alcohol.

What relationships in my life are benefiting from my sobriety?
Reflect on any friendships or family connections that have improved or deepened since you began your journey.

Day 31: Reflection

Today I am grateful for these three things...

1. ______________________________
2. ______________________________
3. ______________________________

Date:

Sober Check in:

What is my intention for today?

____

____

How am I feeling right now?

____

____

Day 32: Reflection

Today I am grateful for these three things...

1. ______________________________
2. ______________________________
3. ______________________________

Date:

Sober Check in:

What is my intention for today?

____

____

How am I feeling right now?

____

____

Day 33: Reflection

Today I am grateful for these three things...

Date:

1. ______________________________

2. ______________________________

Sober Check in:

3. ______________________________

What is my intention for today?

How am I feeling right now?

Day 34: Reflection

Today I am grateful for these three things...

Date:

1. ______________________________

2. ______________________________

Sober Check in:

3. ______________________________

What is my intention for today?

How am I feeling right now?

Day 35: Reflection

Today I am grateful for these three things...

1. ______________________________
2. ______________________________
3. ______________________________

Date:

Sober Check in:

What is my intention for today?

____

____

How am I feeling right now?

____

____

Day 36: Reflection

Today I am grateful for these three things...

1. ______________________________
2. ______________________________
3. ______________________________

Date:

Sober Check in:

What is my intention for today?

____

____

How am I feeling right now?

____

____

Day 37: Reflection

Today I am grateful for these three things...

1. ______

2. ______

3. ______

Date:

Sober Check in:

What is my intention for today?

______

______

How am I feeling right now?

______

______

Day 38: Reflection

Today I am grateful for these three things...

1. ______

2. ______

3. ______

Date:

Sober Check in:

What is my intention for today?

______

______

How am I feeling right now?

______

______

y 39: Reflection

these three things...

Date:

Sober Check in:

What is my intention for today?

How am I feeling right now?

Day 40: Reflection

Today I am grateful for these three things...

1.
2.
3.

Date:

Sober Check in:

What is my intention for today?

How am I feeling right now?

40
DAYS

Day 41: Reflection

Today I am grateful for these three things...

1. ____________________
2. ____________________
3. ____________________

Date:

Sober Check in:

What is my intention for today?

How am I feeling right now?

Day 42: Reflection

Today I am grateful for these three things...

1. ____________________
2. ____________________
3. ____________________

Date:

Sober Check in:

What is my intention for today?

How am I feeling right now?

Day 43: Reflection

Today I am grateful for these three things...

Date:

1. ______________________________

2. ______________________________

Sober Check in: ______

3. ______________________________

What is my intention for today?

____

____

How am I feeling right now?

____

____

Day 44: Reflection

Today I am grateful for these three things...

Date:

1. ______________________________

2. ______________________________

Sober Check in: ______

3. ______________________________

What is my intention for today?

____

____

How am I feeling right now?

____

____

Day 45: Reflection

Today I am grateful for these three things...

1. ______

2. ______

3. ______

Date:

Sober Check in:

What is my intention for today?

______

______

How am I feeling right now?

______

______

Day 46: Reflection

Today I am grateful for these three things...

1. ______

2. ______

3. ______

Date:

Sober Check in:

What is my intention for today?

______

______

How am I feeling right now?

______

______

Day 47: Reflection

Today I am grateful for these three things...

1. ______________________________
2. ______________________________
3. ______________________________

Date:

Sober Check in:

What is my intention for today?

How am I feeling right now?

Day 48: Reflection

Today I am grateful for these three things...

1. ______________________________
2. ______________________________
3. ______________________________

Date:

Sober Check in:

What is my intention for today?

How am I feeling right now?

Day 49: Reflection

Today I am grateful for these three things...

1. ______________________
2. ______________________
3. ______________________

Date:

Sober Check in:

What is my intention for today?

____

____

How am I feeling right now?

____

____

Day 50: Reflection

Today I am grateful for these three things...

1. ______________________
2. ______________________
3. ______________________

Date:

Sober Check in:

What is my intention for today?

____

____

How am I feeling right now?

____

____

50
DAYS

Day 51: Reflection

Today I am grateful for these three things...

1. ____________________
2. ____________________
3. ____________________

Date:

Sober Check in:

What is my intention for today?

How am I feeling right now?

Day 52: Reflection

Today I am grateful for these three things...

1. ____________________
2. ____________________
3. ____________________

Date:

Sober Check in:

What is my intention for today?

How am I feeling right now?

Day 53: Reflection

Today I am grateful for these three things...

1. ________________________________
2. ________________________________
3. ________________________________

Date:

Sober Check in:

What is my intention for today?

How am I feeling right now?

Day 54: Reflection

Today I am grateful for these three things...

1. ________________________________
2. ________________________________
3. ________________________________

Date:

Sober Check in:

What is my intention for today?

How am I feeling right now?

Day 55: Reflection

Today I am grateful for these three things...

1. __________
2. __________
3. __________

Date:

Sober Check in:

What is my intention for today?

How am I feeling right now?

Day 56: Reflection

Today I am grateful for these three things...

1. __________
2. __________
3. __________

Date:

Sober Check in:

What is my intention for today?

How am I feeling right now?

Day 57: Reflection

Today I am grateful for these three things...

1. ____________________
2. ____________________
3. ____________________

Date:

Sober Check in:

What is my intention for today?

How am I feeling right now?

Day 58: Reflection

Today I am grateful for these three things...

1. ____________________
2. ____________________
3. ____________________

Date:

Sober Check in:

What is my intention for today?

How am I feeling right now?

Day 59: Reflection

Today I am grateful for these three things ..

Date:

1. ____________________

2. ____________________

Sober Check in:

3. ____________________

What is my intention for today?

How am I feeling right now?

Day 60: Reflection

Today I am grateful for these three things ..

Date:

1. ____________________

2. ____________________

Sober Check in:

3. ____________________

What is my intention for today?

How am I feeling right now?

60
DAYS

The Radiance Phase (Days 61-90)

What are my proudest achievements during this challenge so far?
Write down at least three accomplishments, big or small, that you've achieved in your sobriety journey.

How has my perspective on social situations changed?
Reflect on your feelings about being in social gatherings. Do you feel more confident, less anxious or empowered in these settings?

What does self-empowerment mean to me now?
Consider how sobriety has changed your view of personal strength. How can you nurture this newfound sense of empowerment in your life?

Day 61: Reflection

Today I am grateful for these three things...

Date:

1. ______

2. ______

3. ______

Sober Check in:

What is my intention for today?

______

______

How am I feeling right now?

______

______

Day 62: Reflection

Today I am grateful for these three things...

Date:

1. ______

2. ______

3. ______

Sober Check in:

What is my intention for today?

______

______

How am I feeling right now?

______

______

Day 63: Reflection

Today I am grateful for these three things ..

1. ______________________
2. ______________________
3. ______________________

Date:

Sober Check in:

What is my intention for today?

____

____

How am I feeling right now?

____

____

Day 64: Reflection

Today I am grateful for these three things ..

1. ______________________
2. ______________________
3. ______________________

Date:

Sober Check in:

What is my intention for today?

____

____

How am I feeling right now?

____

____

Day 65: Reflection

Today I am grateful for these three things...

1. ____________________
2. ____________________
3. ____________________

Date:

Sober Check in:

What is my intention for today?

____

____

How am I feeling right now?

____

____

Day 66: Reflection

Today I am grateful for these three things...

1. ____________________
2. ____________________
3. ____________________

Date:

Sober Check in:

What is my intention for today?

____

____

How am I feeling right now?

____

____

Day 67: Reflection

Today I am grateful for these three things...

1. ______________________________
2. ______________________________
3. ______________________________

Date:

Sober Check in:

What is my intention for today?

How am I feeling right now?

Day 68: Reflection

Today I am grateful for these three things...

1. ______________________________
2. ______________________________
3. ______________________________

Date:

Sober Check in:

What is my intention for today?

How am I feeling right now?

Day 69: Reflection

Today I am grateful for these three things...

1. ____
2. ____
3. ____

Date:

Sober Check in:

What is my intention for today?

How am I feeling right now?

Day 70: Reflection

Today I am grateful for these three things...

1. ____
2. ____
3. ____

Date:

Sober Check in:

What is my intention for today?

How am I feeling right now?

70
DAYS

Day 71: Reflection

Today I am grateful for these three things ..

1. ________________________________
2. ________________________________
3. ________________________________

Date:

Sober Check in:

What is my intention for today?

____

____

How am I feeling right now?

____

____

Day 72: Reflection

Today I am grateful for these three things ..

1. ________________________________
2. ________________________________
3. ________________________________

Date:

Sober Check in:

What is my intention for today?

____

____

How am I feeling right now?

____

____

Day 73: Reflection

Today I am grateful for these three things...

1. ____
2. ____
3. ____

Date:

Sober Check in:

What is my intention for today?

____

____

How am I feeling right now?

____

____

Day 74: Reflection

Today I am grateful for these three things...

1. ____
2. ____
3. ____

Date:

Sober Check in:

What is my intention for today?

____

____

How am I feeling right now?

____

____

Day 75: Reflection

Today I am grateful for these three things...

1. ____________________________________
2. ____________________________________
3. ____________________________________

Date:

Sober Check in:

What is my intention for today?

How am I feeling right now?

Day 76: Reflection

Today I am grateful for these three things...

1. ____________________________________
2. ____________________________________
3. ____________________________________

Date:

Sober Check in:

What is my intention for today?

How am I feeling right now?

Day 77: Reflection

Today I am grateful for these three things...

Date:

1. ____
2. ____
3. ____

Sober Check in:

What is my intention for today?

How am I feeling right now?

Day 78: Reflection

Today I am grateful for these three things...

Date:

1. ____
2. ____
3. ____

Sober Check in:

What is my intention for today?

How am I feeling right now?

Day 79: Reflection

Today I am grateful for these three things...

1. ____________________
2. ____________________
3. ____________________

Date:

Sober Check in:

What is my intention for today?

How am I feeling right now?

Day 80: Reflection

Today I am grateful for these three things...

1. ____________________
2. ____________________
3. ____________________

Date:

Sober Check in:

What is my intention for today?

How am I feeling right now?

80
DAYS

Day 81: Reflection

Today I am grateful for these three things...

1. ____________________
2. ____________________
3. ____________________

Date:

Sober Check in:

What is my intention for today?

How am I feeling right now?

Day 82: Reflection

Today I am grateful for these three things...

1. ____________________
2. ____________________
3. ____________________

Date:

Sober Check in:

What is my intention for today?

How am I feeling right now?

Day 83: Reflection

Today I am grateful for these three things...

1. ______________________
2. ______________________
3. ______________________

Date:

Sober Check in:

What is my intention for today?

____

____

How am I feeling right now?

____

____

Day 84: Reflection

Today I am grateful for these three things...

1. ______________________
2. ______________________
3. ______________________

Date:

Sober Check in:

What is my intention for today?

____

____

How am I feeling right now?

____

____

Day 85: Reflection

Today I am grateful for these three things...

1. ______
2. ______
3. ______

Date:

Sober Check in:

What is my intention for today?

______

______

How am I feeling right now?

______

______

Day 86: Reflection

Today I am grateful for these three things...

1. ______
2. ______
3. ______

Date:

Sober Check in:

What is my intention for today?

______

______

How am I feeling right now?

______

______

Day 87: Reflection

Today I am grateful for these three things...

1. ____________________
2. ____________________
3. ____________________

Date:

Sober Check in:

What is my intention for today?

How am I feeling right now?

Day 88: Reflection

Today I am grateful for these three things...

1. ____________________
2. ____________________
3. ____________________

Date:

Sober Check in:

What is my intention for today?

How am I feeling right now?

Day 89: Reflection

Today I am grateful for these three things...

1.
2.
3.

Date:

Sober Check in:

What is my intention for today?

How am I feeling right now?

Day 90: Reflection

Today I am grateful for these three things...

1.
2.
3.

Date:

Sober Check in:

What is my intention for today?

How am I feeling right now?

90
DAYS

The Golden Horizon Phase (Days 91-100)

What lessons have I learned throughout this 100-day journey?
Reflect on the most important insights or realisations you've gainec during this challenge.

How do I plan to celebrate my achievements over the past 100 days?
Write down at least three ideas for celebrating your commitment to sobriety and the milestones you've reached.

What goals do I have for my life moving forward?
Consider how you want to integrate sobriety into your future. What long-term goals or dreams do you have, and how will sobriety support them?

Day 91: Reflection

Today I am grateful for these three things...

1. ________________________________
2. ________________________________
3. ________________________________

Date:

Sober Check in:

What is my intention for today?

How am I feeling right now?

Day 92: Reflection

Today I am grateful for these three things...

1. ________________________________
2. ________________________________
3. ________________________________

Date:

Sober Check in:

What is my intention for today?

How am I feeling right now?

Day 93: Reflection

Today I am grateful for these three things...

1. ______________________
2. ______________________
3. ______________________

Date:

Sober Check in:

What is my intention for today?

How am I feeling right now?

Day 94: Reflection

Today I am grateful for these three things...

1. ______________________
2. ______________________
3. ______________________

Date:

Sober Check in:

What is my intention for today?

How am I feeling right now?

Day 95: Reflection

Today I am grateful for these three things...

1. ____________________
2. ____________________
3. ____________________

Date:

Sober Check in:

What is my intention for today?

How am I feeling right now?

Day 96: Reflection

Today I am grateful for these three things...

1. ____________________
2. ____________________
3. ____________________

Date:

Sober Check in:

What is my intention for today?

How am I feeling right now?

Day 97: Reflection

Today I am grateful for these three things...

1. ______________________________
2. ______________________________
3. ______________________________

Date:

Sober Check in:

What is my intention for today?

____

____

How am I feeling right now?

____

____

Day 98: Reflection

Today I am grateful for these three things...

1. ______________________________
2. ______________________________
3. ______________________________

Date:

Sober Check in:

What is my intention for today?

____

____

How am I feeling right now?

____

____

Day 99: Reflection

Today I am grateful for these three things...

1. ____________________
2. ____________________
3. ____________________

Date:

Sober Check in:

What is my intention for today?

How am I feeling right now?

Day 100: Reflection

Today I am grateful for these three things...

1. ____________________
2. ____________________
3. ____________________

Date:

Sober Check in:

What is my intention for today?

How am I feeling right now?

100
DAYS

Printed in Dunstable, United Kingdom

66837168R00107